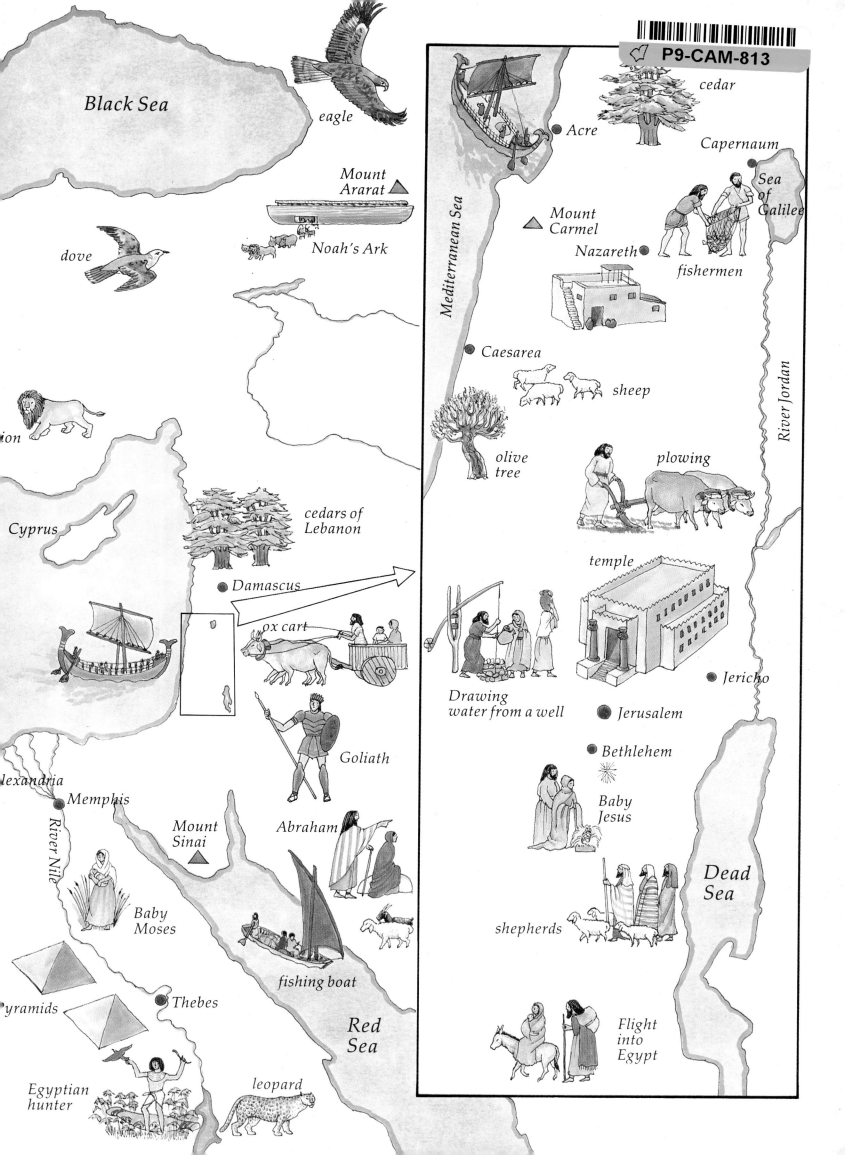

Black Sea

eagle

Mount Ararat ▲

Noah's Ark

dove

lion

Cyprus

cedars of Lebanon

Damascus

ox cart

Goliath

Alexandria

Memphis

River Nile

Mount Sinai

Abraham

Baby Moses

fishing boat

Pyramids

Thebes

Egyptian hunter

leopard

Red Sea

cedar

Acre

Capernaum

Sea of Galilee

Mount Carmel

Nazareth

fishermen

Caesarea

Mediterranean Sea

sheep

olive tree

plowing

River Jordan

temple

Drawing water from a well

Jericho

Jerusalem

Bethlehem

Baby Jesus

shepherds

Dead Sea

Flight into Egypt

First published in USA 1980 by
David C. Cook Publishing Co.
Elgin, IL
Designed and produced by
Grisewood and Dempsey Ltd
141-143 Drury Lane, London WC2
© Grisewood and Dempsey. Ltd., 1980
ISBN 0-89191-339-4
Printed and bound by Vallardi Industrie
Grafiche S.p.A., Milan, Italy

Finding Out about Bible Times

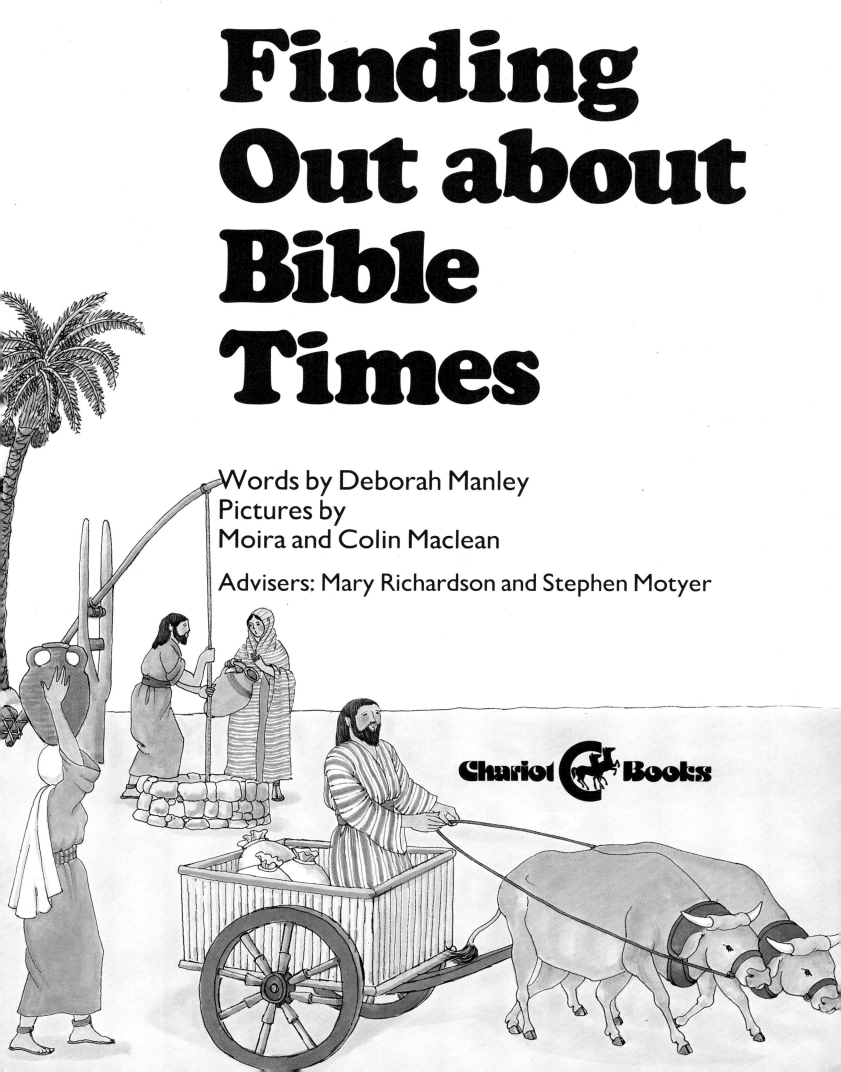

Words by Deborah Manley
Pictures by
Moira and Colin Maclean

Advisers: Mary Richardson and Stephen Motyer

Chariot Books

Contents

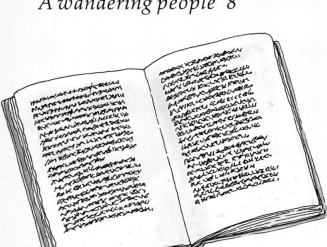

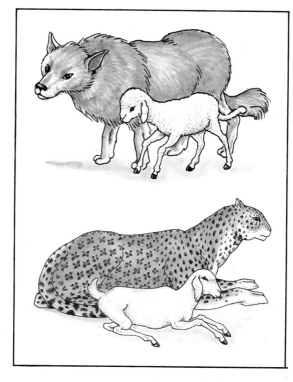

A wandering people

Long, long ago there were people
who lived in the deserts
around the Bible lands.

They were nomads. Nomads are people
who do not live in one place.
They wander to find food and water.

They had flocks of sheep
and herds of goats.
These animals gave them
meat to eat and milk to drink.
The nomads used the wool
and skins for clothes.

The nomads lived in tents
made of goat skins.

They had donkeys
to carry heavy loads.

The nomads wandered in the desert,
looking for water.

Water is very precious in the desert.

Plants grow near water.

When the nomads came to water
they fed their animals.

They collected water
in water-skins for their journey.

Sometimes the water
was far under
the ground.

Sometimes they made wells.
They dug deep
down to find
water.
They lifted the water
out of the well.

A water-skin was made
from a goat skin.

The women carried the water
from the well.

These nomadic people
told stories about
themselves and their God.
We read these stories
in the Bible.

How the Bible was written down

The words of the Bible were written down on scrolls made of skin. They were written in a language called Hebrew. This is the language of the Jewish people.

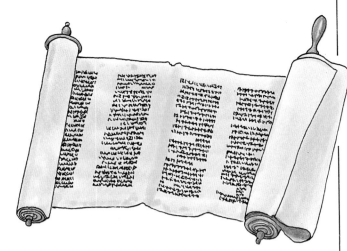

Much later the Bible was translated into Greek and other languages. It was written by hand in books.

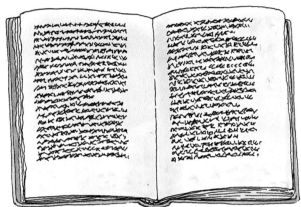

Some Bibles had very beautiful pictures.

About 500 years ago the Bible was printed for the first time. It was printed in Germany by a man called Johann Gutenberg.

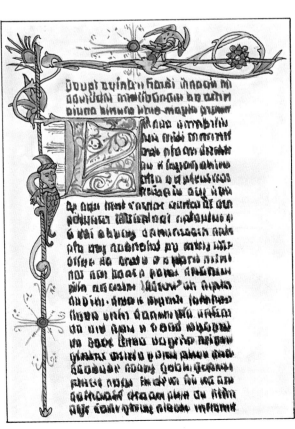

A page from Gutenberg's Bible.

The story of the Bible

The story of the Jewish people begins when God told a man called Abraham to leave his home and find a new land.
God promised that Abraham's people would make a great nation.

The Bible tells stories about Abraham's sons, grandsons and great-grandsons.
His great-grandsons were the makers of twelve great tribes or groups of people.

The Bible tells of a great famine. There was no food in the land.

The Jewish people went to Egypt. They became shepherds and farmers.

pyramids

Life in Egypt

The people of Egypt lived beside the River Nile.
The Nile gave them water for their farms.

People traveled in boats along the river.

People hunted near the river.

A pharaoh going hunting.

A king of Egypt was called a pharaoh.
When a pharaoh died, he was buried in a huge tomb. The tomb was called a pyramid.

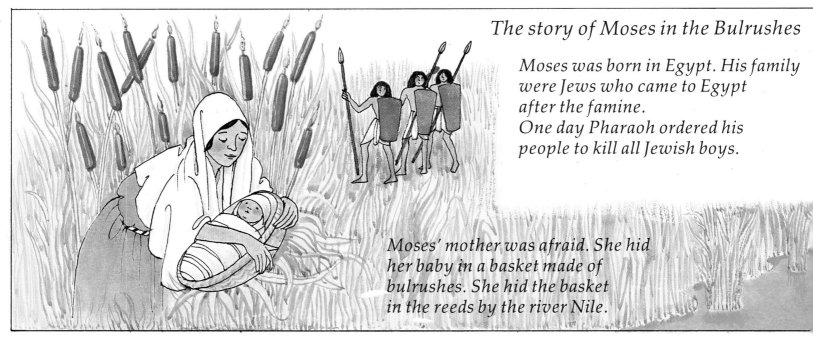

The story of Moses in the Bulrushes

Moses was born in Egypt. His family were Jews who came to Egypt after the famine.
One day Pharaoh ordered his people to kill all Jewish boys.

Moses' mother was afraid. She hid her baby in a basket made of bulrushes. She hid the basket in the reeds by the river Nile.

The Egyptians painted many pictures.
We know a lot about them from their pictures.

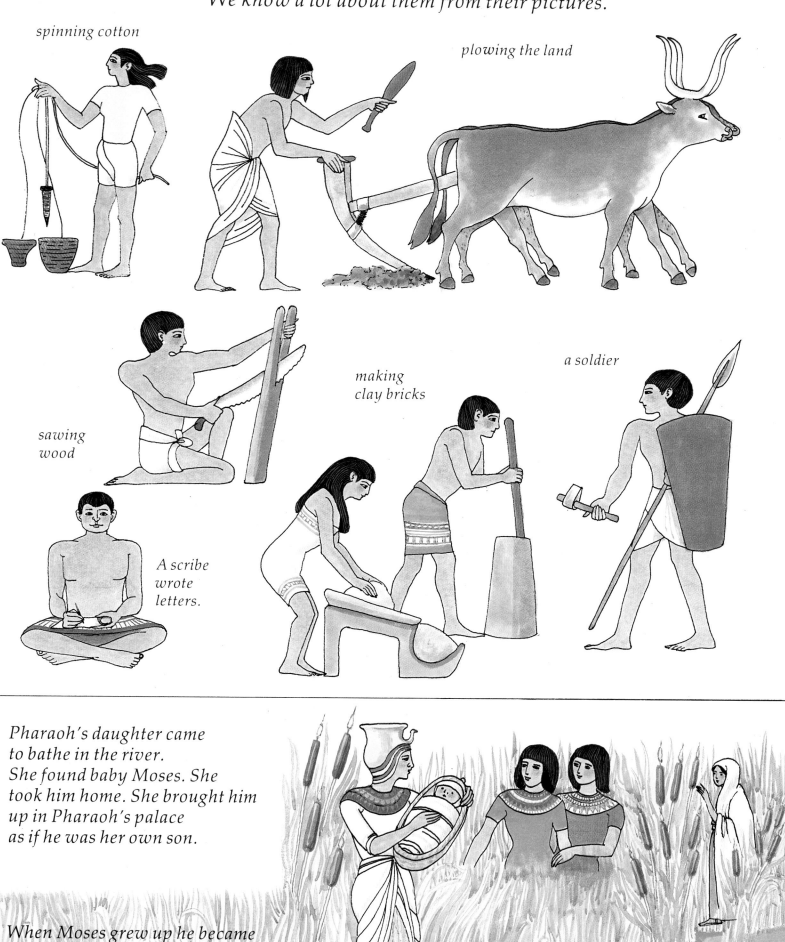

spinning cotton

plowing the land

sawing wood

A scribe wrote letters.

making clay bricks

a soldier

Pharaoh's daughter came to bathe in the river. She found baby Moses. She took him home. She brought him up in Pharaoh's palace as if he was her own son.

When Moses grew up he became a leader of the Jews. He led his people out of Egypt.

The story continues

One of the pharaohs or kings
of Egypt made the Jews
into slaves.
They had to work very hard
and they were not paid.

Then Moses led them
out of Egypt.
The waters of the Red Sea parted.
Moses led them through.
He led them across the Red Sea.
Then the waves closed behind them.
The pharaoh's soldiers could not follow.

Moses led his people
into the desert.
He led them to a mountain
called Sinai.
There God spoke to Moses.
He promised to protect
the Jewish people.
He gave them rules to live by.
These rules are called
the Ten Commandments.

At last the Jewish people
found a new home.
They settled down. They built
a city called Jerusalem.
That city is still there today.

Now the Jewish people wanted a king.
One of their kings was called David.
He started life as a shepherd boy.

David's son was called Solomon.
When he became king he built a
great temple in Jerusalem.

Later the temple was destroyed.
The Jewish people had many, many troubles.
They were taken away to a land called
Babylon. They were made slaves again.

Then, at last, they returned
to the home that God had promised
to Moses and his people.

How David became King

David was a shepherd boy. He had seven
brothers. They lived in a village
called Bethlehem.

One day a man called Samuel came
to Bethlehem.
God had told Samuel to choose one of
the brothers to be the future king
of the Jews.

Samuel said that David, the youngest,
would be king.

David did not become king for a long time.
He lived in the palace of King Saul.
He made Saul happy by playing to him on his harp.

What is a sling?

Shepherds like David
used slings to protect
their sheep from
wild animals.
A sling is made of
leather. Stones can be
thrown from it.

Soldiers in Bible times

They carried shields.

Saul's army had to fight the army of a people called the Philistines. One of the Philistines was a giant called Goliath. Everyone was afraid of Goliath.

Goliath said that if anyone defeated him, the Philistines would stop fighting.

David said he would fight Goliath. He killed the giant with a stone from his sling.
The people were delighted. David became their hero.

Later, when Saul died, David became the king of the Jewish people.

They used bows and arrows.　　They used swords and spears.　　Their leaders went in chariots.

How people traveled

Ordinary people went on foot. They walked and carried their loads.

Oxen drew carts.

Donkeys carried people and their loads.

Rich people had carriages.

A chariot was faster than a carriage.

Camels carried loads in the desert.

The story of Noah and his Ark

God was very angry with all the bad people in the world. God told a good man called Noah that he was going to make a great flood. The water would cover all the land. God told Noah to build a big boat called an Ark.

God told Noah to take two of every animal into the Ark. Noah took the animals into the Ark.

Ships carried cargoes
and passengers at sea.

Rich people rode
horses.

Some people were carried
in litters by their servants.

Oxen were strong,
but they were slow.

Some people had wagons to carry heavy loads.

When the flood came everyone was drowned.
But the Ark floated on the water and
Noah and his family were saved.
God sent a rainbow as a sign that the waters
will never again cover the Earth.

What people wore

Making woolen clothes

Shepherds herded sheep on the hills.

The sheep were washed to clean their wool.

The wool was combed to straighten it.

The wool was spun into thread on a spindle.

The thread was woven on looms to make cloth.

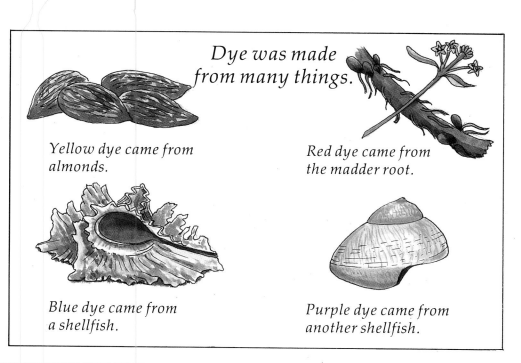

Dye was made from many things.

Yellow dye came from almonds.

Red dye came from the madder root.

Blue dye came from a shellfish.

Purple dye came from another shellfish.

You can dye cloth with onion skins.

The wool was sheared from the sheep.

The wool was dyed in vats.

The cloth was made into clothes.

Joseph's coat of many colors

Joseph was the favorite son
of a shepherd called Jacob.
Jacob made his son a special coat of many colors.
Joseph's brothers were very jealous of this coat.
They thought Joseph was too proud.
They threw him into a pit in the desert.
Then they dipped his coat of many colors in blood.
They told his father that Joseph had been killed.
Some merchants found Joseph.
They took him to Egypt and sold him as a slave.
Later Joseph helped the king
of Egypt to understand what his dreams meant.
Then Joseph became a leader in Egypt.

People at work

Most people in Bible times were farmers.
Some people lived in towns and villages
and did other work.

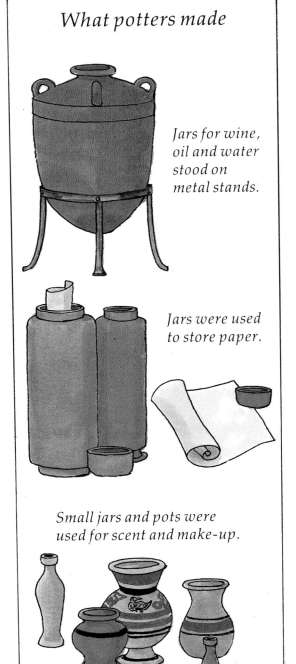

What potters made

Jars for wine, oil and water stood on metal stands.

Jars were used to store paper.

Small jars and pots were used for scent and make-up.

Metal workers made tools and pans.

Potters made clay pots.

In the markets, merchants sold the things other people made.

People who built

carpenters

brickmakers

stone masons

Some men were soldiers.

Scribes did all the writing.

Some people made music.

Fishermen caught fish in the lakes and rivers.

Who made these things?

Weighing and measuring

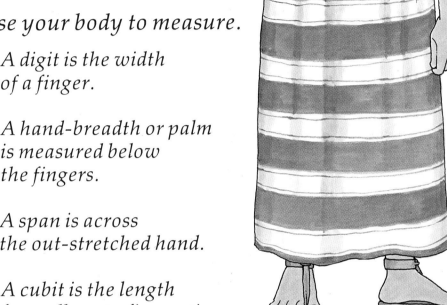

In Bible times people used different ways to measure and weigh things.
Try using their weights and measures.

Measure it yourself

Goliath was 6 cubits and a span tall. How tall was he? How tall are you?

Noah's Ark was 300 cubits long.
Can you measure that?

4 digits = 1 palm
3 palms = 1 span
2 spans = 1 cubit

Use your body to measure.

a. A digit is the width of a finger.

b. A hand-breadth or palm is measured below the fingers.

c. A span is across the out-stretched hand.

d. A cubit is the length from elbow to finger-tip.

Merchants used balances to weigh things.

Land was measured by how much a pair of oxen could plow in a day.

Three kinds of money were used in Bible times.

The shekel was a Jewish coin.

Liquid measures

Liquid measures were named after the size of the container.

A bath was just over 2 quarts.

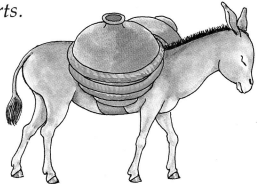

A kor was 10 baths or one donkey load.

The drachma was a Greek coin.

The denarius was a Roman coin.

Shekel was the word for "to weigh".

Make your own balance.

You need: 2 yogurt pots
a coat hanger
some string

Suspend the two pots with string from the coat hanger.
Balance the hanger on your finger.
Weigh things in the pots.

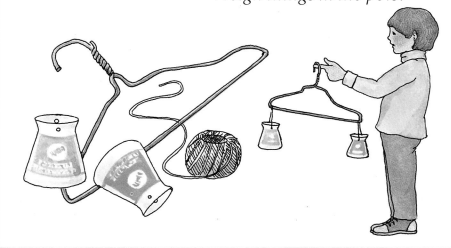

The temple of Solomon

In early Bible times the people prayed
to God in a tent. It was called the tabernacle.
They carried the tabernacle with them on their journeys.

King Solomon decided to build a Temple in Jerusalem.
This Temple would be the new House of God.

The Temple was built of stone.
The walls were paneled
with cedar wood from
the Lebanon.

The priests washed
their hands and feet
in this huge brass basin
before going into
the Temple.
It was called a laver.

The laver

The Holy Place

Porch

The temple of King Solomon
was destroyed
after about 400 years.
All the gold
was taken away
from Jerusalem.

The altar of
burnt offering

The priests sacrificed
animals on the altar
of burnt offering.

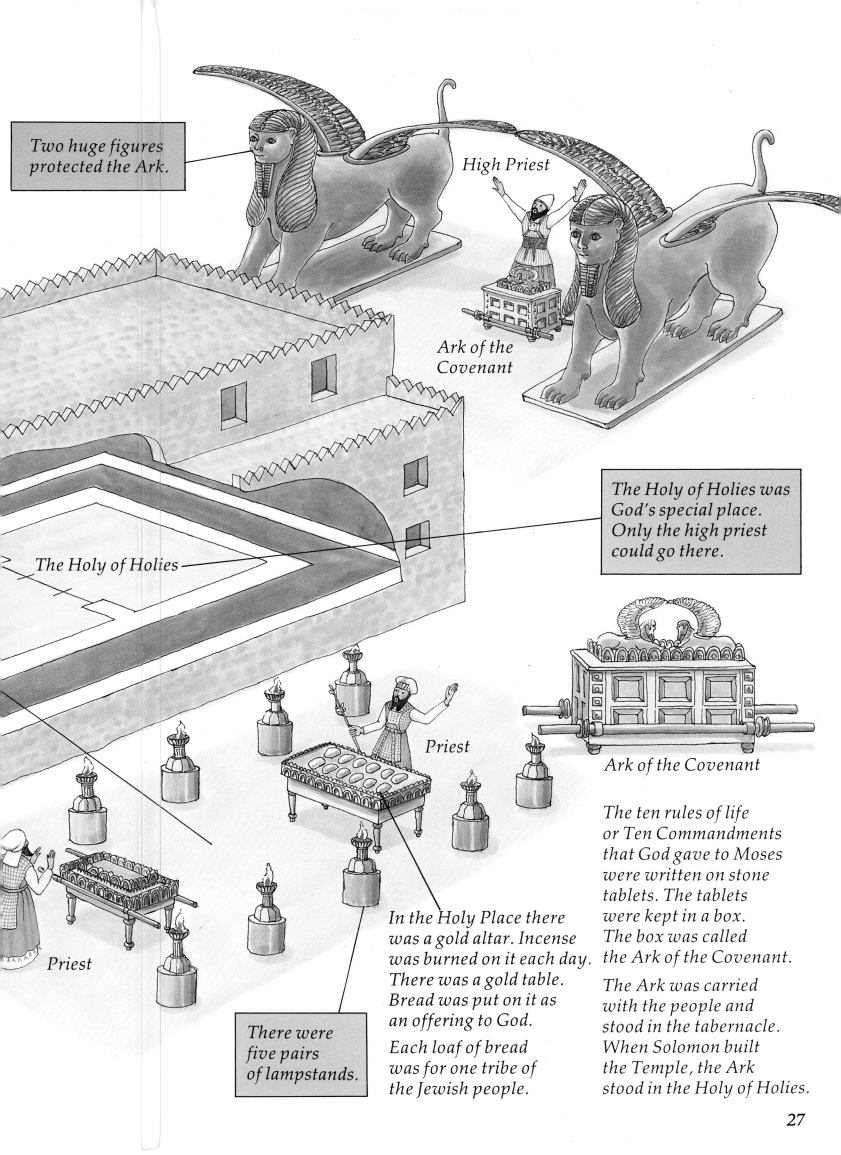

Two huge figures protected the Ark.

High Priest

Ark of the Covenant

The Holy of Holies was God's special place. Only the high priest could go there.

The Holy of Holies

Priest

Ark of the Covenant

In the Holy Place there was a gold altar. Incense was burned on it each day. There was a gold table. Bread was put on it as an offering to God.

Each loaf of bread was for one tribe of the Jewish people.

Priest

There were five pairs of lampstands.

The ten rules of life or Ten Commandments that God gave to Moses were written on stone tablets. The tablets were kept in a box. The box was called the Ark of the Covenant.

The Ark was carried with the people and stood in the tabernacle. When Solomon built the Temple, the Ark stood in the Holy of Holies.

Rome comes to the Bible lands

The Romans were a very powerful people.
They conquered many lands.
They conquered the Bible lands too.
They joined all the lands together
into the Roman Empire.

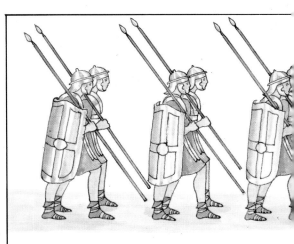

The Roman army was very stro[ng]
The foot soldiers had swords,
spears and shields.

Rich Romans
lived in
beautiful
houses
called villas.

a litter

Roman ships
carried cargoes
around the
Empire.

a cart

They built aqueducts
to carry water.

a chariot

The Romans built very good roads.
Some of them are still used today.

Some Roman bridges
are still used.

The Romans built good roads so their armies could travel quickly.

Each group of 100 soldiers was led by an officer called a centurion.

Some Roman soldiers rode horses.

The Romans built temples for their many gods.

a water wheel

The Romans ruled their Empire very strictly.
Each part of the Roman Empire had a ruler called a governor.

The boyhood of Jesus

Jesus was born in a village
called Bethlehem.
The story of Jesus's birth
is always told at Christmas.

The story tells how
an angel told Mary that
she would have a son.
He would be the son of God.
The angel said that Mary
should call him Jesus.

Joseph and Mary went to Bethlehem.
The village was very crowded.
They had to sleep in a stable.
Baby Jesus was born there.

Three shepherds followed a bright star.
It led them to Baby Jesus.

Three wise men saw the bright star too.
They followed it to Jesus.

Herod the King heard of Jesus.
He feared that Jesus would become
powerful. He ordered that all
baby boys in Bethlehem should be killed.

But Joseph and his family fled to Egypt.
When Herod died they returned.

Jesus grew up in the village of Nazareth.
Joseph was a carpenter. The house they
lived in may have looked like this.

The family used
the roof like an
extra room.

The staircase
went up the outside
wall to the roof.

The carpenter's shop
was part of the house.

The women
ground corn
to make bread.

Water was kept
in a jar.

The women cooked
the food outside.

There was only
one room in
the house.

The work of Jesus

When Jesus grew up, he taught people about God.

One day he saw two fishermen. He asked them to join him. They became his first followers or disciples.

Jesus told stories to people about God.
He healed sick people.
People were astonished by his work.
They traveled very far to see him.

Jesus rode into Jerusalem on a donkey.
People put palm leaves on the ground
for him to ride over. They called him
their new king.

The priests of the temple
were angry. They wanted
to kill Jesus.

One of his disciples
was called Judas.
He helped the priests
to capture Jesus.

Jesus was taken away
and hanged on a cross.

Afterwards Judas was very sorry.
It was too late. Jesus was dead.

The farming year

A farmer in Bible times worked very hard.
He and his family worked all year round.

1: The farmer plowed the land
before the rain came.

2: Then he scattered the seeds.

3: The family planted vegetables
near the house.

4: When the plants grew,
they hoed away the weeds.

5: The children tended
the sheep and goats.

The story of the sower

Jesus told a story about a
farmer sowing grain.

Some seeds fell on the path.
The birds flew down and ate them.

Some seeds fell on stony ground.
Plants grew, but there was
no water, so they died.

6: When the grain ripened, the farmer harvested it. He used a sickle to cut the grain.

7: He separated the grain from the straw.

8: When the harvest was in, it was time to feast.

9: Then the grape vines needed care. Soon the fruit was ready.

10: Then the olives were harvested. By now it was time to plow the land again.

Some seeds fell on thorny ground. The thorns choked the plants.

Some seeds fell on good earth. There the plants grew well. The farmer had a good crop.

Jesus said this was like God's words. Some people did not listen. Some listened, but did nothing. Yet others listened and did what God said.

The plants of the Bible lands

The plants that grew in Bible times still grow in the Bible lands today.

Wood from the great cedars of Lebanon was used to build Solomon's temple. Today the cedar is shown on Lebanon's flag.

The olive tree gives olives for food and oil for lamps.

The vine gives fresh grapes for food. Grapes are dried in the sun to make raisins. Wine is made from the grapes too.

Dates come from the date palm. The palm fronds are used for roofing and matting.

Figs grow on the fig tree.
They are eaten fresh or
sun-dried.

Bread is made from wheat and
other cereals.
Loaves in Bible lands
were flat.

Linen cloth was made from the leaves
of the flax plant.

Weaving cloth
from flax.

The papyrus reed
grows along the
River Nile.
It was used
to make paper.

Have a Biblical meal.

Make a meal from flat bread,
fresh grapes, dried fruit,
cream cheese, onions, and
cucumber.
Drink milk or water.
Sweeten your food with honey.

Creatures of the Bible

These animals lived in the Bible lands.
The Bible speaks about them.
It often compares people to animals,
and looks forward to a world of love and peace.

Your father and his men are
enraged. They are like a bear
robbed of her cubs
in the field.

(2 Samuel 17:8)

Can the Ethiopian change
his skin or the leopard his spots?

(Jeremiah 13:23)

Behold he comes
leaping upon the mountains,
bounding over the hills.
My beloved is like a gazelle
or a young stag.

(Song of Solomon 2:8-9)

Jesus said: Beware of false
prophets, who come to you
in sheep's clothing, but
are really ravenous wolves.

(Matthew 7:15)

Oh that I had
wings like a dove!
I would fly away
and be at rest.

(Psalms 55:6)

There shall the owl
nest and lay
and hatch and gather
her young
in her shadow.

(Isaiah 34:15)

And not
a sparrow is
ever forgotten
by God.

(Luke 12:6)

They shall mount up
with wings
like eagles.

(Isaiah 40:31)

The wolf shall dwell
with the lamb.

The leopard shall lie
down with the kid.

The lion shall eat straw
with the ox.

The cow and the bear
shall feed. Their young
ones shall rest together.

The calf and the lion
and the sheep shall
live together, and
a little child shall
lead them.

(Isaiah 11:6-7)

Other stories Jesus told

Jesus sometimes taught people by telling them stories. These stories showed people what Jesus believed.

Stories like these are called parables. Here are some of the parables Jesus told.

The King and his Servant

The king's servant owed him money. He could not pay. He begged the king for mercy.

The king forgave him.

But another man owed the servant money. The servant had him put in prison.

The king was very angry. He had his servant put in prison until he could pay his debts.

Jesus said God would naut forgive people unless they forgave others.

The Good Samaritan

A man was traveling when he was attacked by thieves. They beat him and took his clothes.

The Wise and Foolish Maidens

A man was to be married. Ten maidens went to meet him. They each had a lamp. Five of them were foolish. They had no oil in their lamps. Five were wise. They took plenty of oil.

40

Other travelers saw him.
They did not stop.
They passed by on the other side
of the road.
Then a Samaritan traveller
saw the man. He washed his
wounds. He took him to an inn
to rest.

Jesus said that everyone
should be like the good
Samaritan and help other people.

The Lost Sheep

A shepherd who has a hundred
sheep loses one.
He leaves the ninety nine and
searches for the lost one.
He is very happy when he finds it.

Jesus said that God too is pleased
when one bad person becomes good.

The bridegroom was late. It grew dark.
The maidens fell asleep.
When the bridegroom arrived the
foolish maidens had to get oil.
They missed the wedding.
Jesus said people should always be
prepared.

How the message was carried

After Jesus was killed, he appeared to his disciples. He told them to go out and tell people about what he had taught.

Peter led the disciples to carry Jesus's message. Many people came to hear them, and believed what they said.

The Romans did not like what the disciples said. They were very cruel to people who believed in Jesus.

There was a man called Paul. He hated Jesus's teachings. Then one day he was travelling to Damascus. Jesus appeared and spoke to him. Then Paul believed in Jesus.

Paul traveled all over the world telling people about Jesus.

Paul wrote letters to people who believed in Jesus. The letters helped them to understand the message of Jesus.

The story of Jesus and how his message spread is told in part of the Bible called the New Testament.

How we know about Bible times

The people of the Bible lived a
very, very long time ago.
So how do we know about them
and how they lived?

Much from the past is buried
under the ground.
New towns were built over
old ones.
But people called archeologists
dig to find the past.

They wrote on leather
scrolls. The scrolls
were stored safely.
Some of them can be
read today.

People painted pictures
Here is an ancient Egyptian picture.
It was painted on a wall.
It shows craftsmen at work.

The craftsmen are making things
from wood and metal.
One man is writing. One man is weighing.

Archeologists at work
and what they find

The things they find tell us
about the people who lived
long, long ago.

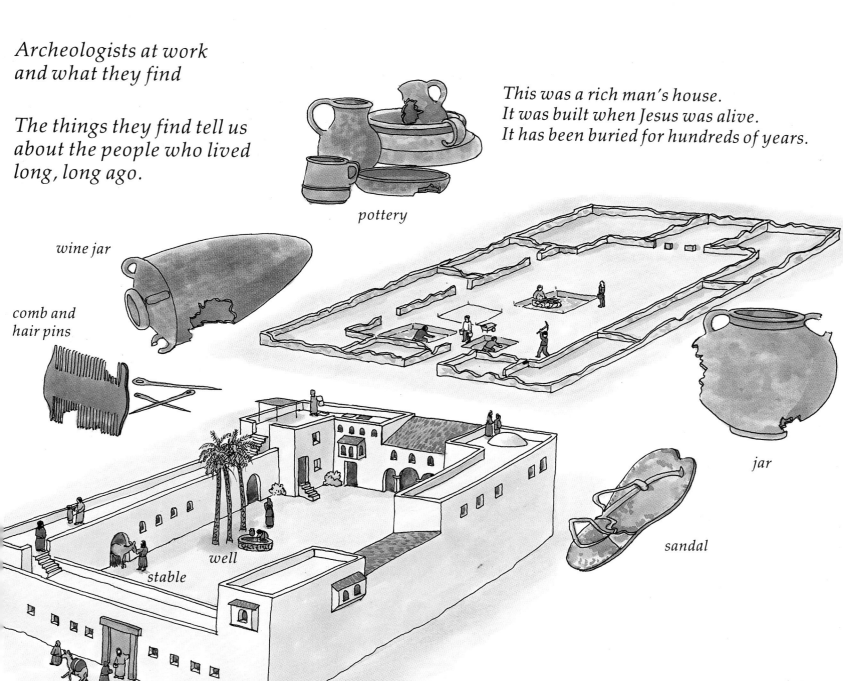

pottery

This was a rich man's house.
It was built when Jesus was alive.
It has been buried for hundreds of years.

wine jar

comb and
hair pins

jar

sandal

stable

well

gateway

This is what the rich man's house looked
like long ago
when Jesus was alive.

The things that archeologists find

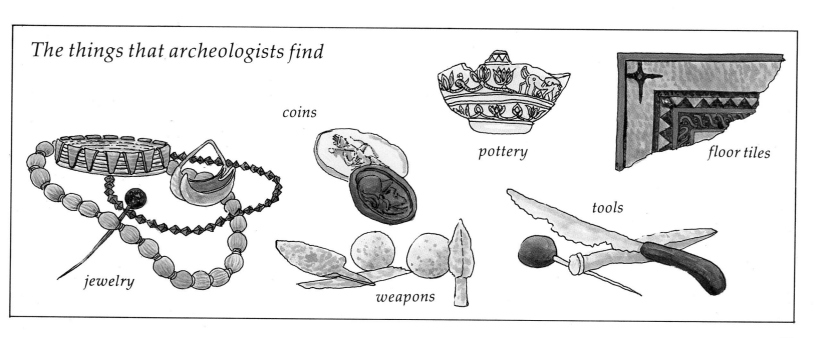

coins

pottery

floor tiles

tools

jewelry

weapons

wolf

Italy

owl

Coliseum

Adriatic Sea

Rome

chariot

Parthenon

Roman
ship

Greek ship

Athens

Greece

Sicily

Crete

Mediterranean Sea

Egyptian
ship

palm trees

Egyptian wor

The lands of the Bible